EXPLORING CORAL REEFS

Coral Reef
Adventure

by Glen Phelan

What is the largest animal home? Maybe an eagle's nest. Some are almost 3 meters (10 feet) across. A termite mound? Some are 9 meters (30 feet) high! But those animal homes are nothing compared to homes built by **coral polyps.** Many coral polyps are no larger than a pencil eraser, yet they build **coral reefs,** the largest animal homes on Earth. Some reefs are so big they can be seen from space! How do animals so small build something so big?

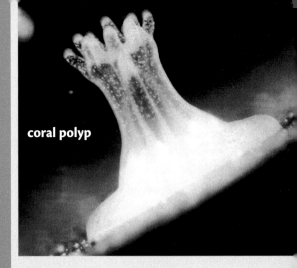
coral polyp

Most coral polyps form colonies. Thousands of polyps live in these colonies. Reef-building coral polyps have soft bodies, but they each form a hard outer skeleton. When they die, their skeletons remain. Then young polyps attach themselves to those skeletons and form their own. Do you see the pattern? Each generation of polyps grows on top of the previous generation. Layer by layer, a rocky coral reef builds up.

Coral Reef Facts

- A coral polyp uses its tentacles to sting tiny animals drifting by. The tentacles then bring this food into the polyp's mouth.

- Reef-building corals have another source of food. Tiny algae live inside a coral polyp's body. Like plants, algae get energy from the sun. They use the energy to make sugars. The polyps use some as food.

- Different kinds of algae give coral polyps different colors.

- Algae depend on sunlight. So reef-building corals grow best in shallow water where sunlight reaches the ocean floor.

- Coral reefs form in warm, clear water.

- Coral reefs build slowly. Most are 5,000 to 10,000 years old. Some have been forming for millions of years.

- Coral reefs have an amazing variety of life. Only tropical rain forests have more **biodiversity.**

Exploring Types of Reefs

Coral reefs form a type of **ecosystem.** An ecosystem includes all the living and nonliving things in an area and how they interact. Coral reefs are fascinating ecosystems. Let's explore three reefs around the world.

Palmyra Atoll

The first is in the middle of the Pacific Ocean. It's the Palmyra **Atoll.** An atoll is a reef around a shallow lagoon. At Palmyra, sand collected and built up above the water's surface. Birds nest in the plants there. Large coconut crabs climb trees. But it's a whole different world just beneath the waves. Let's strap on our scuba gear and dive in.

∨ Palmyra Atoll

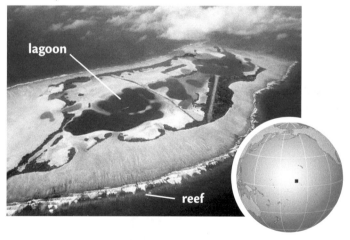

lagoon

reef

grouper

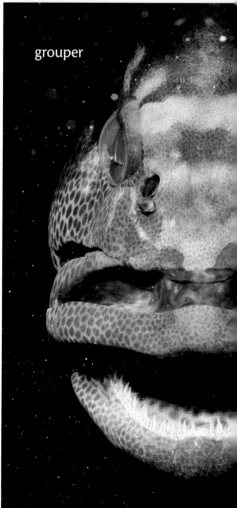

> This grouper blends into the reef. It waits until fish swim nearby. Then it swallows its food in one gulp.

4

humphead parrotfish

Like many reef fish, the humphead parrotfish has body parts with **adaptations** for eating certain foods. It uses its big head to break coral into pieces. It uses its teeth to crush the coral. Then it can get at the algae and polyps inside. The ground-up coral leaves the fish's body. It becomes sand and washes up on the atoll beaches.

Butterflyfish have small snouts. They stick out. This makes it easier for them to peck at coral polyps and other tiny animals.

butterflyfish

Red Sea Fringing Reef

Now we head west to the shores of the Red Sea. Here reefs form an edge, or fringe, along the shore. Most **fringing reefs** grow against the shoreline. Others form just offshore. All of them are exciting to explore.

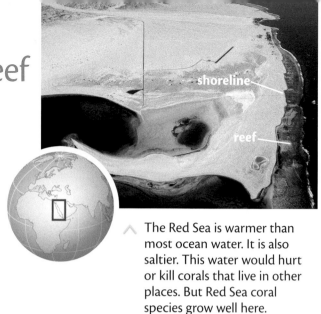

shoreline

reef

The Red Sea is warmer than most ocean water. It is also saltier. This water would hurt or kill corals that live in other places. But Red Sea coral species grow well here.

Don't touch this odd fish! The lionfish's large spines are poisonous. They warn predators to stay away.

lionfish

Picasso triggerfish

∧ Suppose you made a model of a fish. Suppose you painted it with lots of colors and patterns. It might end up looking like this Red Sea beauty.

∨ What's one big difference between fish in a reef and fish in the open ocean? Color! Most open-water fish are silvery or blue-gray. Many reef fish have bright colors. Colors and patterns help fish blend in with the corals. This adaptation helps them hide from predators.

yellowtail tang

Belize Barrier Reef

Now let's travel to the coast of Belize. This Central American country borders the Caribbean Sea. Let's explore the Belize **Barrier Reef.** A barrier reef stretches along a coast. This type of reef can form a barrier to ships and large waves. But it's not a barrier to divers! Let's take a look.

A school of butterflyfish swims by. A queen angelfish nibbles on a coral. Everything seems peaceful. Suddenly a reef shark races toward the angelfish. The angelfish makes a quick turn and hides. The shark looks for a meal somewhere else.

The Belize Barrier Reef is the largest barrier reef in the Northern Hemisphere. It's 260 kilometers (161 miles) long.

queen angelfish

Many reef fish have a flattened body, like a pancake on its side. Look at this queen angelfish. It's body is built for quick movements and sudden stops. It hides between rocks and coral. Its body shape is an adaptation that helps it escape from predators.

A reef shark is built for speed. Its streamlined shape helps it swim at high speeds. So do its powerful tail and fins. Tuna, swordfish, and many other fish in the open ocean also have these adaptations.

reef shark

Name That Coral

You could spend years exploring reefs. But you would see only a little of their amazing biodiversity. About 700 kinds of corals and 4,000 kinds of fish live in reefs. Would you like to name some of these corals? Don't worry, it's fun. Many corals are named by the way they look. Try to match these corals with their names. The answers are shown at the bottom of the page, but no peeking!

A. brain coral   **B.** elkhorn coral   **C.** great star coral   **D.** lettuce coral

E. orange cup coral   **F.** sea fan coral   **G.** staghorn coral   **H.** table coral

1. Polyps live on both sides of this coral's "leaves."

2. Its branches can grow up to 2 meters (6.5 feet) long.

3. The polyps of this coral are huge—the size of a thumb.

4. Most kinds of coral colonies live a few decades. This one lives up to 900 years.

5. The shape of this coral exposes as much of the surface as possible to sunlight.

6. This kind of coral is also called sun coral.

7. This is a soft coral because it does not have a hard limestone skeleton.

8. This fast-growing coral grows 5 to 10 centimeters (2 to 3.9 inches) per year.

Check In How are different reef fish adapted to life in coral reef ecosystems?

THE GREAT BARRIER REEF

by Glen Phelan

Reef Relationships

What do the Grand Canyon and the Great **Barrier Reef** have in common? They're among the seven natural wonders of the world. Have you ever seen the Grand Canyon? It's spectacular. And so is the Great Barrier Reef!

What's so special about the Great Barrier Reef? It's the largest reef system in the world. And it's the largest structure built by living organisms. This collection of about 3,000 reefs is over 2,000 kilometers (1,250 miles) long. It's located off the northeastern coast of Australia.

The Great Barrier Reef has incredible **biodiversity.** So far scientists have identified about 400 types of corals and more than 1,500 types of fish there. Scientists are discovering new organisms all the time. You never know what you'll find in the reef.

Great Barrier Reef World Heritage Area

INDIAN OCEAN

AUSTRALIA

Coral Sea

Great Barrier Reef

Canberra

Sydney

Melbourne

Tasman Sea

N W E S

0   300   600 Miles
0   300   600 Kilometers

COMPETITORS AND PARTNERS

The Great Barrier Reef looks like a garden. But it's a battleground for the organisms that live there. Algae compete for sunlight. Fish and other animals compete for food, shelter, and mates. Organisms use physical and behavioral **adaptations** to beat their competitors. These adaptations cause unusual interactions.

Saddled butterflyfish feed on algae. But they also like sea anemones. Butterflyfish are not affected by the poisonous sting of the anemones' tentacles. They tear the tentacles off and eat them. What chance do the anemones have? Clownfish to the rescue! Clownfish are immune to the anemone's poison. They live among the anemone's tentacles. They drive the butterflyfish away. The clownfish's bright colors also attract smaller fish. The anemone stings, paralyzes, and eats the fish. The clownfish eats the scraps. Clownfish and anemones are partners in this watery world.

Speaking of partners, the bluestreak cleaner wrasse is the best. It uses its markings and movements to attract fish that need to be cleaned. Larger fish let the wrasse nibble its parasites. Wrasses get a meal. The other fish get rid of their parasites. This is one of the many partnerships at the Great Barrier Reef.

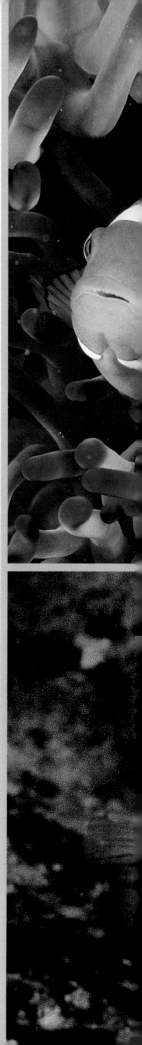

A clownfish swims without harm among the stinging tentacles of a sea anemone.

A butterflyfish uses its pointed mouth to poke into small spaces in search of food. It also might snag a tentacle from a sea anemone.

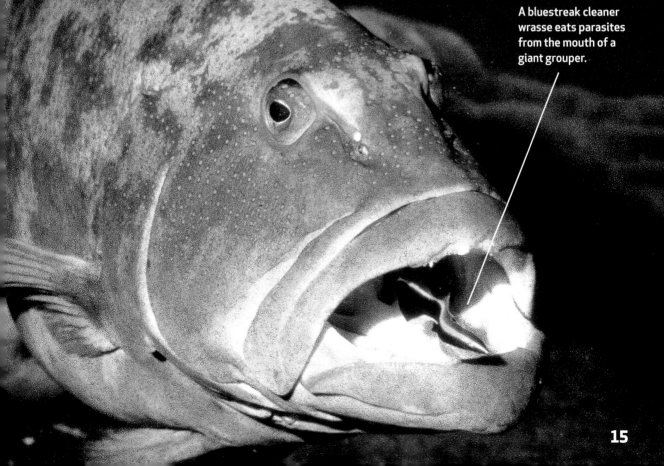

A bluestreak cleaner wrasse eats parasites from the mouth of a giant grouper.

EAT OR BE EATEN

Hold your palms close to your face. Do you feel heat? Believe it or not, you are feeling the sun's energy. Plants use the sun's energy to make food. We get energy from the sun when we eat plants or animals that eat plants. Your body uses that energy to keep your cells working, to move, and to keep warm.

Organisms in the Great Barrier Reef also depend on the sun for energy. Energy enters the ecosystem through plant-like plankton, algae, or plants. Then it passes from one organism to another. The result is a **food web** that shows what eats what. This diagram shows some of these feeding relationships.

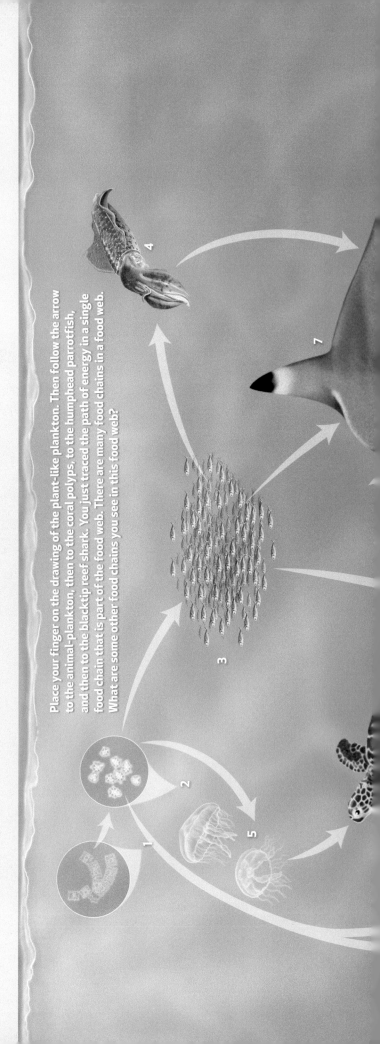

Place your finger on the drawing of the plant-like plankton. Then follow the arrow to the animal-plankton, then to the coral polyps, to the humphead parrotfish, and then to the blacktip reef shark. You just traced the path of energy in a single food chain that is part of the food web. There are many food chains in a food web. What are some other food chains you see in this food web?

1. plant-like plankton
2. animal-like plankton
3. blue sprat
4. reef squid
5. moon jelly
6. hawksbill sea turtle
7. blacktip reef shark
8. day octopus
9. sponge
10. regal angelfish
11. humphead parrotfish
12. crown-of-thorns sea star
13. staghorn coral
14. brain coral
15. coral polyps
16. mantis shrimp
17. sea urchin
18. titan triggerfish
19. algae

Check In Describe three examples of relationships on the Great Barrier Reef.

GENRE Personal Narrative

Read to find out about two snorkeling trips to the Belize Barrier Reef.

Snorkeling in Belize

by Joe Baron

Samantha Brown Goes Snorkeling

Can you imagine getting paid to travel all over the world? Samantha Brown is the host of a television travel program. She shows her viewers amazing places. Whenever I watch her show, I want to see those places for myself. In one episode, Samantha took a snorkeling trip to the Belize **coral reef.** Her guide was Alfonse Graniel. He had grown up snorkeling and diving at the reef. And he's been showing people the wonders of the reef for many years.

Samantha told her viewers that the Belize coral reef is the second largest **barrier reef** in the world. Alfonse explained that the coral reef is made of living organisms. Over time, the corals grow to the surface of the water. They've been there for hundreds of years.

Samantha and Alfonse arrived at the snorkeling site. Then Samantha told her secret: she was afraid to dive in! Alfonse said that it was very safe. He said that they would see lots of fish, maybe even nurse sharks. He assured Samantha that it was safe to swim with the nurse sharks, even though they have sharp teeth. Samantha was worried, but she was reassured to see that Alfonse still has two legs, two arms, and all of his fingers.

A nurse shark glides above the coral at the Belize Barrier Reef. Nurse sharks do not usually harm people. Other sharks can be dangerous.

Alfonse dove in first. Finally, SPLASH! In Samantha went. Alfonse pointed out five nurse sharks nearby. Samantha laughed and screamed at the same time. He told her to take calm, slow breaths through the snorkel. Soon Samantha was gliding in the water. With Alfonse guiding her she experienced some of the best snorkeling in the world. Alfonse had been coming to the reef since he was twelve years old. He knew some of the reef inhabitants personally, and they seemed to know him. Samantha called Alfonse "The Fish Whisperer" as he calmly held a ray in his arms. Samantha worked up the courage to stroke the ray.

Alfonse lives in San Pedro Town in Belize. He introduces many people to the wonders of the Belize Barrier Reef.

Alfonse carefully approaches a ray.

Alfonse helped Samantha feel comfortable around the sharks. He carefully approached a shark and gently held it in his arms. He told Samantha the shark was safe to pet. Samantha reached out and patted the shark. She ran her hand along its belly and then along the top of its head. She thought of the old saying that you have to face your fears, but she didn't expect to give one a hug! As she held the shark, she thought that it was like a big puppy! Then she turned to Alfonse and they shared a high-five. Samantha had faced her fears, and she had a great snorkeling experience!

> *"She thought of the old saying that you have to face your fears, but she didn't expect to give one a hug!"*

A nurse shark swims with horse-eye jacks. These are just a few of the fish that can be seen at the reef.

Joe Baron Goes Snorkeling

I didn't go snorkeling until I was an adult. It was like being dunked into a tropical fish tank! In my adventures, I have startled a baby octopus, fed tuna to hungry rays, and been bonked on the head by a barracuda.

Like television travel host Samantha Brown, I joined a group led by Alfonse Graniel. We boarded Alfonse's boat along with another guide, Giovanni. On our way to the reef, I asked Alfonse about any scary times on his snorkeling trips. He told of a snorkeler taking a picture of a shark. SNAP! The shark snatched the camera out of the man's hands! The man was so scared he ran right across the surface of the water. I began to wonder about Alfonse's stories.

It is important that you can see clearly through your mask. It must fit properly so water does not flow in.

The sea fan is one of many types of corals found at the Belize Barrier Reef.

Alfonse said that you can see the **coral polyps** feeding at night if you carry a bright light. Alfonse said it's easy not to be afraid. If you see something scary in the dark, just turn off your light. You won't see it anymore. I wondered a little more about Alfonse's stories.

At the reef, Alfonse gave instructions: Keep your body horizontal. That will get you close to the coral without harming it or yourself. Also, you must have a clear view through your mask. Giovanni began scrubbing my mask. He said he was using something that would not scratch it. I asked what it was. "Can you keep a secret?" he asked. "Yes", I said. "So can I," he replied. What a joker. Later, I saw a piece of dead sea fan in his hand. So that was the scratch-free material! But no one will ever know. I can keep a secret, too.

One more thing about your mask, you spit in it! Then you rub the spit around. This helps keep the mask from fogging up underwater.

Finally, it was time to get in the water. I spit, put on my mask, and put on my brand new fins. They felt kind of tight. I leaned over the edge of the boat, and SPLASH! There was bright green sea grass all around me. It was a short swim to the corals. Alfonse pointed out many amazing animals. I snapped pictures of colorful fish and corals, and a sea turtle. We even got a close-up look at a nurse shark.

All too soon, it was time to go back to land. We climbed aboard the boat. Alfonse announced that someone had snorkeled with the plastic inserts in his fins. You're supposed to remove them before you put the fins on your feet. We all had a big laugh. But I can tell you, it's uncomfortable when you leave those things in when you're snorkeling!

Alfonse and a swimming companion, a horse-eye jack

A sea turtle paddles by the sea grass near the reef.

On the way back to land, I laughed again when someone stepped on the handle of a fire extinguisher. A cold, white cloud puffed up at the bottom of the boat. Okay, I was the one who stepped on the handle. It will be our little secret.

As we motored back to land, the sun and the spray behind the boat made a rainbow. We were back in San Pedro Town before we knew it. What a trip! The weather was perfect, but the underwater world of the reef was incredible. And on this trip, I got to hold a nurse shark. Next time I'll go snorkeling at night. But I will keep the light on!

"What a trip! The weather was perfect, but the underwater world of the reef was incredible."

Joe and a new friend, a nurse shark

Check In   How were the two snorkeling trips alike and different?

Saving
Coral Reefs
by Joe Baron

Coral reefs are in danger and people must protect them. Why? Coral reefs are valuable. Millions of people who live near coral reefs depend on tourism for jobs. Local economies depend on money tourists spend. Coral reefs are important in other ways too. **Barrier reefs** slow down waves and keep coasts from being worn away. About one quarter of all marine life depends on coral reef habitats. Millions of people have jobs and food because of the lobster, fish, and shrimp that live in the reefs.

In the tourist season that ended on June 12, 2012, about 1.92 million visitor-days were spent in Australia's Great Barrier Reef Marine Park. People travel to the reef for diving, snorkeling, boating, and scenic flights.

Coral reefs have a great variety of living things, or **biodiversity.** This makes coral reefs valuable to people. Many reef organisms produce chemicals. Some of them are used to make medicines for people. Chemicals from sea sponges are used to make a drug used to treat leukemia, a type of cancer. Toxin from cone snails is used to make a painkiller. More medicines are being developed. Some will treat asthma and arthritis. Others will treat infections and heart disease. Some people refer to coral reefs as "the medicine cabinets of the 21st century."

Lost or abandoned fishing nets can harm coral reefs and animals that live there. Overfishing is a problem at some coral reefs.

Blast fishing kills fish and destroys sections of the coral reef.

A crown-of-thorns sea star eats coral polyps. These sea stars cause much damage to coral reefs.

The activities of people are damaging coral reefs. People near and far from the ocean can add to the problem. They burn fossil fuels such as coal, oil, and natural gas. These fuels add greenhouse gases to the atmosphere. This causes climate change. The oceans get warmer. Then the **coral polyps** push out the helpful types of algae that live in their bodies. These algae provide coral with some of their food. Without the algae, the polyps have less food. The coral look white. This is called coral bleaching.

Fertilizers and pesticides can get into rivers and then the ocean. Pollution from fertilizers can cause overgrowth of harmful types of algae that smother coral polyps. This pollution can increase the number of crown-of-thorns sea stars that eat the polyps. Soil that is washed into the ocean can settle on the reef. This keeps polyps from getting light and nutrients.

People near or in the water also can harm the reefs. Some people walk on the coral. Others take coral from the reefs. Some boaters drag their anchors on the reefs. Some people fish in ways that wipe out the fish and damage the reefs.

Unusually warm water can cause coral bleaching. Sometimes corals can recover. If the conditions are severe, the corals may die.

About a third of the world's coral reefs are dying. About one-tenth of them are already dead. Experts say that three quarters of Earth's coral reefs might be gone by 2050. There are things people can do so that we can enjoy these amazing reefs for a long time.

This diver is using cyanide, a poison, to stun reef fish. Cyanide harms many organisms of the coral reef. Cyanide fishing is illegal in many places. The laws are often not well enforced.

What can YOU do to HELP SAVE coral reefs?

✚ Conserve water. The less you use, the less pollution gets into the ocean.

✚ Walk, bicycle, or ride a bus. This reduces pollution produced from cars. Plant trees to reduce greenhouse gases.

✚ Don't eat fish that are overfished at coral reefs. Look for lists of recommended seafood on the Internet.

✚ If you visit a coral reef, be responsible. Don't touch the reef. Don't take samples. Anchor boats away from the reefs.

✚ Tell people about coral reefs and how to protect them. Support groups that create marine protected areas.

Check In What do you think is the most important reason for saving coral reefs?

Discuss

1. What information in "Coral Reef Adventure" helped you better understand the other three pieces in the book?

2. Describe the differences between an atoll, a fringing reef, and a barrier reef.

3. Describe how energy from sunlight is transferred through a food web in the Great Barrier Reef.

4. In "Snorkeling in Belize," what are some details that make the two snorkeling experiences different from each other?

5. What are some types of pollution that affect coral reefs? How are coral reefs affected by these types of pollution?

6. What do you still wonder about coral reefs and how to protect them? What research could you do to find out more?